VISION BOARD
CLIP ART BOOK
FOR BLACK WOMEN

Everyone needs a well thought-out vision for their life.
Your life's map to success is your vision.

This book will help you create your vision so you can
achieve your dreams, aspirations and what fulfills you.

 # YOUR FREE GIFTS

As a way of saying thanks for your purchase,
I want to offer you two free bonuses:

FREE GIFT #1:

"86 QUICK & EASY STRATEGIES FOR SAVING MONEY" EBOOK

Discover 86 practical and easy-to-implement strategies to save money, budget wisely, and achieve your financial goals. This eBook is a valuable resource for securing your financial future.

FREE GIFT #2:

"CREATING YOUR DREAM LIFE WITH YOUR OWN VISION BOARD" COURSE

Unlock the potential within you and start manifesting your aspirations with my exclusive vision board course. Set clear intentions and turn your dreams into reality.

SIGN UP FOR MY EMAIL NEWSLETTER TO GET INSTANT ACCESS:

FREEBIES.KALISHIAWINSTON.COM

You will also get weekly tips, free book giveaways, discounts, and so much more.

All of these bonuses are completely free and come with no strings attached. You do not need to provide any personal information except for your email address.

EAT less SWEET

I look 👓 GOOD because I drink WATER

CAREER	BUSINESS	HOME
CREATIVITY	WEALTH	GOALS
FITNESS	FUN	HEALTH
WELLNESS	FINANCE	SAVINGS
SPIRITUALITY	MINDSET	FAMILY
EDUCATION	HOBBIES	PERSONAL GROWTH
MANIFEST	SCHOOL	TRAVEL
GIVING BACK	SELF CARE	LOVE
PETS	MENTAL HEALTH	COMMUNITY
ADVENTURE	KIDS	FAITH
LIFESTYLE	SELF LOVE	FRIENDSHIP

things to see	focus	luxury
dream job	independent	progress
successful	my dream life	believe
wedding	goals to meet	take risks
dreamer	less screen time	study
boss	calm	gratitude
every day	create	live simply
profit	things to try	love your life
experiences	beautiful	outdoors
imagine	hope	grateful
joy	explore	get it

luxury	focus	things to see
progress	independent	dream job
believe	my dream life	successful
take risks	goals to meet	wedding
study	less screen time	dreamer
gratitude	calm	boss
live simply	create	every day
love your life	things to try	profit
outdoors	beautiful	experience
grateful	hope	imagine
get it	explore	joy

I WILL SPEAK KINDER TO MYSELF

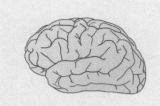

MY MENTAL HEALTH IS JUST AS IMPORTANT AS MY PHYSICAL HEALTH

I AM COMFORTABLE IN MY OWN SKIN

I EMBRACE SUCCESS

I LIVE A RICH AND ABUNDANT LIFE

I WILL RECEIVE THE ENERGY THE UNIVERSE PRESENTS ME

I WILL NOT LET SOCIETY DICTATE WHO I AM

I AM PROUD OF MY CULTURE

I ACCEPT RESPONSIBILITY FOR MY HAPPINESS AND DEVELOPMENT

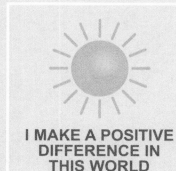

I MAKE A POSITIVE DIFFERENCE IN THIS WORLD

I LOVE WHO I SEE WHEN I LOOK IN THE MIRROR

I CONTROL & CREATE MY FUTURE

NO MATTER WHAT, I WILL ALWAYS LOVE ME FOR ME

STRESS LESS

DREAM **BIG**

TAKE THE FIRST STEP

Never give up

DO MORE OF WHAT YOU LOVE

FOCUS ON Your Goals

SAY YES to new adventures

MILLIONAIRE.

I AM CREATING THE LIFE OF MY DREAMS

YOU MAKE YOUR OWN LUCK

YOUR WISHES COME TRUE

Follow your heart

DON'T WISH FOR IT, WORK FOR IT

LONDON	PERU	MEXICO
AFRICA	ITALY	SWEDEN
GREECE	CUBA	IRELAND
CROATIA	MOROCCO	AUSTRALIA
MALDIVES	SPAIN	BORA BORA
PARIS	BERLIN	MOSCOW
CANADA	RIO DE JANEIRO	CHINA
ASIA	EUROPE	JAPAN
SCOTLAND	NEW YORK	PRAGUE
HONG KONG	AMSTERDAM	DUBAI

BANK OF THE UNIVERSE

DATE:

PAY TO THE
ORDER OF:

$

DOLLARS

FOR:

00000000 &56   00000000 296 456

BANK OF THE UNIVERSE

DATE:

PAY TO THE
ORDER OF:

$

DOLLARS

FOR:

00000000 &56   00000000 296 456

BANK OF THE UNIVERSE

DATE:

PAY TO THE
ORDER OF:

$

DOLLARS

FOR:

00000000 &56   00000000 296 456

THANK YOU

"Helping others is the way we help ourselves."
-Oprah Winfrey

Have you ever given without expecting anything in return? If you have, you are aware of the tremendous rewards that can come from helping others. Not because it makes you a better person, but because it makes you feel good to know that you were able to improve someone else's life in some small way.

I want to give you this chance and ask you for a favor. In order for me to accomplish my mission of inspiring my readers to live their best lives, I first have to reach them. And the majority of people do evaluate a book based on its reviews. So, could you please take 3 minutes to post your honest review of this book on Amazon? With your help, this book will reach more people and assist them in achieving their goals and dreams. Just find this book on Amazon and write a few short words (or long words, I won't judge).

P.S. If you believe this book will benefit someone you know, please let them know about it too.

To your success,

Kalishia Winston